Living Well

Living Well

Scriptural Reflections for Every Day

Joan Chittister

ORBIS BOOKS

Maryknoll, New York 10545

Photo credits:
John Argauer, M.M.: pp. 6, 12, 112, 124
Mev Puleo: p. 26
Megan McKenna: pp. 38, 50, 76, 88, 100
Eric Wheater: p. 62
John Beeching, M.M.: p. 136
Catherine Costello: p. 149

Second printing April 2001

The Catholic Foreign Mission Society of America (Maryknoll) recruits and trains people for overseas missionary service. Through Orbis Books, Maryknoll aims to foster the international dialogue that is essential to mission. The books published, however, reflect the opinions of their authors and are not meant to represent the official position of the society. To obtain more information about Maryknoll or Orbis Books, please visit our website at http://www.maryknoll.org.

Published in 2000 by Orbis Books, P.O. Box 308, Maryknoll, NY 10545-0308

Originally published as *The Monastic Way 1999* by BENETVISION, Erie, PA 16503

Manufactured in the United States of America

Library of Congress Cataloging-in-Publication Data

Chittister, Joan.
    [Monastic way]
    Living well : scriptural reflections for every day / Joan Chittister.
      p. cm.
    ISBN 1-57075-320-2 (pbk.)
    1. Devotional calendars – Catholic Church. 2. Bible – Meditations. I. Title.
BX2170.C56 C45 2000
242′2. – dc21

                                00-034673

This book is dedicated to Kathleen Hartsell Stephens,
a living well of patience and generosity,
whose depth of soul and steady presence is long-time gift.

Introduction

One of the most ancient teachings of the monastic life is that silence is a necessary aspect of spiritual development. The function of silence is not to cut us off from the rest of the world simply for the purpose of cutting us off. No, the function of silence is to enable us to listen to what is going on inside ourselves. It is only in silence that we can discover what noise it is in us that makes it so difficult for us to hear the quiet voice of God within. Until we allow ourselves some silence, it is impossible to hear.

The irony is that there is very little that is silent about silence. Inside ourselves is a very noisy place. It is so often full of clanging, grinding, crying congeries of thoughts in confusion, thoughts in contradiction, thoughts in tension. The cavern of the heart is the resting place of the fears and angers of a lifetime. In there we find the seedbed of every aching ambition, every unspoken frustration, every unnoted response. Down deep within the corners of the soul is the self-talk that tells us who we are and what we think about the world around us and what we're worrying about and what we're struggling with and what we're confused about and what we fear. Down there in the rills and recesses of our unspoken ruminations is the repository of the noisy self.

Clearly, the key to living well is not so much what's outside of us as what's inside of us. It is what is deepest within us, not what is most vexing around us, that determines the quality of our lives. That's why we have to fill ourselves with thoughts that give substance to our relationships, perspective to our memories, wisdom to our daily decisions, and spirit to our hearts.

Everything that's in the heart we either put there or allow to nest there. *We* are responsible for the content of our souls.

These reflections on fragments of scripture are simply an attempt to grapple with the ideas under the ideas. They are meant to be the stuff of a new heart.

My suggestion is that you memorize the scriptural quotation of the month and bring your own silent dialogue to it. As you wrestle with the ideas here, which are intended only to prompt your own reflections, you will certainly see the sounds of silence within you turn color, become brighter, and bring you to the point where you find yourself thinking differently and living well.

January

Wisdom 1:14

*The creative forces of the world make for life;
there is no deadly poison in them.*

I was in France for a meeting that was far too heavy and way too long. Clearly someone had made a mistake: there was one afternoon left free on the schedule. The question was an obvious one. What one thing could anyone do in Paris that would tap the essence of the society, touch the heart of the culture, walk into the soul of the city? In Paris, the answer had to be art.

I had never been in the Louvre, one of Europe's oldest and most prestigious art galleries, which sits in the center of Paris, holds one of the largest collections of great art in the entire world, and is an eye into the best time has to offer. It is room after room after room of wall-size paintings, larger-than-life sculptures, period furniture, and collections of the masters in wide-open galleries. Tucked into an alcove on the landing of a back stairway, defended only by a thin blue velvet rope, stood a Rembrandt on a low easel. A Rembrandt. Sitting there. Unguarded. Uncovered. Unchained. Close enough to touch. Low enough to pick up and carry off. "Where are the guards?" I asked our guide. "Isn't this dangerous to have a painting like this sitting here open in a back stairway? I could just pick that up and carry it out." And *the guide smiled. "Oh, but not at all, Madame," she said. "If you took that painting under your arm, every scullery maid in France would chase you. Art is our national inheritance. We would guard it with our lives."*

I tried to imagine what our national inheritance is in the United States. I thought of bombs and rockets, computers and cars. And winced. I wonder if we would defend beauty?

January 1: Art is the imagination unleashed on the world to make it a more seeking, more sensitive place.

January 2: Imagination asks, "What's possible?" Technology asks, "What works?" The question is, What is the more important question? Alice Embree says, "America's technology has turned in upon itself; its corporate form makes it the servant of profits, not the servant of human needs." No wonder the world looks like it does.

January 3: "Imagination is the eye of the soul," Joseph Joubert says. To give the world soul, then, we will have to develop imagination. If you want the world to change, every day imagine something different and say it aloud so others can come to imagine it too. Then before you know it, the climate of change will reach critical mass.

January 4: Technology is a measure of the complexity of the social system. Art is a measure of the human soul. Georges Braque says of it: "Art upsets, science reassures."

January 5: A world without art is a world without vision. Erich Fromm says of the situation: "The danger of the past was that people became slaves. The danger of the future is that people may become robots."

January 6: Don't be afraid to think differently than other people. Be afraid only if you're not thinking at all about anything of human importance. Or, as Sydney Harris wrote, "The real danger is not that computers will begin to think like people, but that people will begin to think like computers." Human imagination is a faculty that needs nurturing if we are ever going to get beyond the robotization of the human race.

January 7: Beauty breaks open the human soul to what is possible in the face of the impossible.

January 8: Imagination breaks open the human mind to what is desirable when what is real is unacceptable.

January 9: "Technology," Max Frisch says, "is the knack of so arranging the world that we don't have to experience it." Beauty, on the other hand, is the spirituality of hope in the midst of alienation. When we identify, respond to, and cultivate the beautiful, experience becomes a symphony to be celebrated, not a dirge to be avoided.

January 10: Beauty is a beacon on the mountain of the mind that brings us home to our best selves.

January 11: Beauty is the face of God looking at Itself.

January 12: Beauty brings with it the realization in the midst of struggle, in the depths of darkness, in the throes of ugliness, that the best in life is, whatever the cost, really possible.

January 13: We are a prose- and profit-oriented people, a bread-and-butter culture. What we may need most in the next millennium is a population of poets. When the poet speaks, the subject matter is always the voice of the heart crying out for attention in a darkened room. The rest of us know what's in the room, of course, but only the poet says what it really means. "Poetry," Gwendolyn Brooks says, "is life distilled."

January 14: When we come into contact with what is beautiful, we reframe our vision of the world. Then everything ugly, squalid, tawdry, cheap, or garish begins to look like what it really is. Next to the flash of the radiantly true and the deeply insightful, ugliness is exceedingly boring.

January 15: What makes a thing ugly, garish, and cheap? Excess. Always excess. When something is too gaudy, too ornamented, too loud, too anything, it is always ugly. Which would be fine if ugliness weren't a worm that corrupted our spirits as well as our tastes in music, clothes, and movies. "Nothing in excess," the ancients called it. Everything "just right," we call it.

January 16: When ugliness seeps in, we confuse what is effective with what is right.

January 17: Beauty is a deeply spiritual experience. It shouts to us always, "More. There is yet more to life than we have yet to know."

January 18: Bloodless and dull repetition of great art ought to be a federal offense. It desensitizes the soul to those moments in time when enlightenment, understanding, insight come like a flash because someone saw them before we did and enabled us see them as well.

January 19: Before cameras, television, airplanes, and computers, artists were the only touch we had with the elsewhere, the other, the foreign. Now they are the only touch we have with the meaning that underlies the situation. Or as Paul Klee puts it, "Art does not reproduce the visible; rather it makes it visible."

January 20: When a sense of beauty is not cultivated in a people, any degree of barbarity is possible.

January 21: When there is too much noise, too much color, too many curlicues, too much posturing, too garish a shape, too intrusive an element, too self-centered a presence, beauty has been prostituted for spectacle.

January 22: "Computers can figure out all kinds of problems," James Magary writes, "except the things in the world that just don't add up." The memory of the Holocaust, the sight of the geography of evil in South Africa, the genocide in Bosnia, the trivialization of women the world over, the disregard for children everywhere as we pursue power and profit in a patriarchal world, demand that we ask again the questions, What is it to be fully human? and, How do we develop it? At a moment in history in which the destruction of the planet and the extinction of people have been raised to high art, to levels beyond the realm of human imagination only sixty years ago, those may be the core questions of the twenty-first century. And beauty may be their answer.

January 23: How can we save the human soul unless we resuscitate the human imagination? Imagination allows us to rethink everything we ever knew, to start over one more time, to begin again, to dare to be new, to encapsulate the old in brave new ways. "A rock pile ceases to be a rock pile," wrote Antoine de Saint-Exupéry, "the moment a single person contemplates it, bearing within the image of a cathedral."

January 24: The artist is the eye of a blind world.

January 25: A great deal passes for imagination today that could never have been possible before the advent of computer models, movie sets, and "paint by number" kits, however popular such things may be. The fact is that what is copied is not art; it is, at core, craft. What is not spiritually penetrating — meaning a new way of seeing things — is not art. It is at best formula fiction. What is simply more of the same — no uniqueness intended, no gasp of realization arrested in mid-flight — is not art. It is at best a cartoon character of life lived without the inner cleansing that comes with a shocking consciousness of the present moment.

January 26: Art is the sacrament of awareness, a trumpet call to every soul to come to life again and see, to rise to the heights of itself again and become, to strive for more than the lowest level of existence, and to transcend the banal.

January 27: "The highest spiritual intention," John Cassian writes, "is one of contemplating beauty." Why? Because it is only the raising of the mind to humanity's highest aspirations that can save a world in technological danger.

January 28: We are a people with more commitment to function than to soul. We want things to work rather than to be. So we buy plastic flowers instead of real ones and spend our money instead on cement for parking lots.

January 29: There are cures for deprivation of spirit: We could take down the billboards that turn the land-scape into a junkyard of ideas. We could refuse to allow people to turn marble statues into plastic replicas. Or we could simply own one soul-shattering piece of art our-selves — a one of its kind made by someone who cared enough to be original — and put it up in a solitary place over and against the commonplace that surrounds us. We could let it seep into the center of the self until we find that we can never be satisfied again by visual clichés, until we realized that only the true is really beautiful. Then the whole world would begin to see again.

January 30: We cannot hope for fullness of life without nurturing fullness of soul. Where we are must be more beautiful than it was before our coming.

January 31: The beauty and imagination we do not nourish within ourselves cannot exist in the world around us because we are its microcosm. We cannot moan the loss of quality in our world and not ourselves seed the beautiful in our wake. We cannot decry the loss of the spiritual and continue to function only on the level of the expedient. If we are to have a world of music, poetry, art, and beauty, we must develop the best of those in our own lives.

February

1 JOHN 4:12

If we love one another,
God lives in us,
and God's love is perfected
in us.

I t was the week before Christmas and I was driving across town only half listening to one of a plethora of Christmas programs that crowd the airwaves every holiday season. This one was about the pressure on seasonal producers, the people who make fruitcakes and gingerbread houses and gift packages of cheese and jellies, to meet demands and make the shipping deadlines that are so essential to the success of their businesses. One company spokesperson after another told stories of company crises barely averted — of having to label jam jars by hand and getting refrigerator bags from meat dealers in the early hours of a late December morning in order to mail perishables by dawn. Nice angle, I thought, and drifted into one of those fugue states where radios play but no one hears them.

But all of a sudden I found myself totally alert. Here was a real record: a maker of fruitcakes whose family had been in the business for 115 years was talking. The company, he was telling a radio audience of millions, had never turned a customer away in its entire history. "Well, I take that back," he corrected himself. "There was one time. During the hostage crisis in the Middle East," he

24

said, "someone wanted to send a fruitcake to the Ayatollah Khomeini. We refused the order." The voice had
a triumphant ring to it. Christmas music up, commercial in, program over, the strains of "O Little Town of
Bethlehem" still ringing in our ears.

I admired the person who ordered that fruitcake. I
grieved for the person who had refused the order. In
that one gesture, the Gospel went by the wayside in the
name of patriotism and business and the birth of Christ.
What can the rest of the year possibly be like when its
peak moments, its most Christian indicators, are clouded
by conflict and self-righteousness and national chauvin-
ism? What happens to human community when ego and
unkindness take over? Not the Gospel, that's for sure.

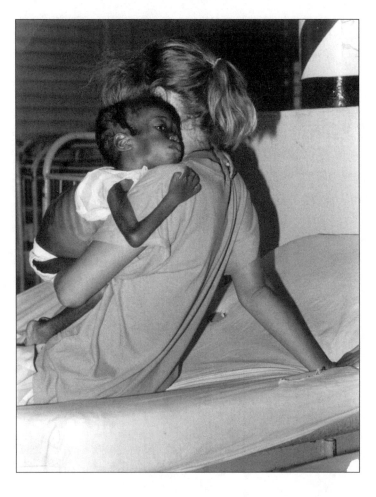

February 1: Imagine how many conflicts could be resolved, how much community could be restored, by one word of concern, one gesture of kindness, for the other person. In fact, imagine how many of your own personal relationships would be different than they are if we ourselves had ever interrupted our own narcissism with real love. It almost hurts to think about it.

February 2: "If you stop to be kind, you must swerve often from your path," Mary Webb wrote. The truth is that most kindness interrupts our personal agendas. Kindness is what we do when we should be doing something else.

February 3: Kindness is a type of love. There is such a thing as good business, fine manners, cultivated civility. Who hasn't seen it? But kindness is not doing what we should; kindness is doing what we don't need to do for someone who has no right and no intention to demand it. Then community happens automatically.

February 4: The reason we defend ourselves so vociferously and judge others so unkindly is because we know better than anyone else how really little there is to defend in us. To mask our own limitations we so often, so unkindly, degrade others and destroy the bond of community among us.

February 5: Loving others the way they need to be loved is so different from loving them the way we demand to love them. The one kind of love frees; the other entraps. The one kind lasts; the other breaks from the weight of its own insatiable demands. The first kind is for sake of the other and strengthens the bond between us in the process; the second kind of love is meant to satisfy ourselves.

February 6: Community and conformity are two different things. Community nourishes us to become great individuals in the midst of a nurturing group. Conformity requires us to become just like everyone else to such a degree that no one can ever really become anything.

February 7: "Call it a clan, call it a network, call it a tribe, call it a family," Jane Howard writes. "But whatever you call it, whoever you are, you need one." When we drum anyone out of the community for which we have responsibility to care, we have contributed to the downfall of the world.

February 8: "What if they gave a war," the poster says, "and no one came." The point is plain and terrible: the world dissolves into wrack and ruin because somewhere along the line, at moments both common and crucial, we forgot to love. But what we don't love, God can't solve.

February 9: It's imperative to remember that what God loves, God loves through us.

February 10: To refuse prejudice, to measure the human race one person at a time, is to weld the world into love.

February 11: Two things obstruct love: judgment and fear. When we begin to realize that there is more to everything than we shall ever know, when we begin to approach every person on the street trustingly, the city, the neighborhood, the family changes. Then we become like the person who sends fruitcake to the Ayatollah Khomeini.

February 12: "The love of our neighbor in all its fullness," Simone Weil wrote, "simply means being able to say, 'What are you going through?'" There is nothing that melts the heart more quickly than the voice of someone who really cares about what you're dealing with, how it's affecting you, what you need to bear it. Try it sometime and watch what happens to the way people begin to relate to you too.

February 13: If we really care about someone, we do something that shows it. Anything else is talk.

February 14: There is absolutely no way that we can come to holiness without coming to love. All the principles, all the legal scorecards in the world won't do it. Why? Because we were made by Love and can be saved only by Love as well.

February 15: It is our love that makes the love of God present. As outbursts of the love of God, we are God's love on earth.

February 16: The love we lack inside ourselves is the measure of our own spiritual underdevelopment. No need to wonder, then, how close we are to sanctity.

Everything we do gauges it. The only question we need to ask is, For what purposes, in what spirit, and for whose sake did we do everything we did today?

February 17: "Kindness gives birth to kindness," Sophocles said. Ever wonder why people treat you the way they do?

February 18: We recognize the value of kindness especially when it is lacking: when the clerk snaps at us, when the bus driver closes the door in our faces, when we need help and no one volunteers. Then the role of kindness in holding the world together becomes all too plain.

February 19: "True kindness," André Gide says, "presupposes the faculty of imagining as one's own the suffering and joys of others." Kindness isn't only help in a time of need; it is consciousness in a time of isolation, joy at a time of celebration, concern at a time of separation as well. Kindness makes someone else's agenda our own.

February 20: People give millions of dollars worth of aid to hurricane victims. People also applaud marauding armies and inhuman penal systems. The real shock to the human heart is to discover that a world that can be so kind can also be so brutal. How is it that self-righteousness can so easily overcome understanding?

February 21: The real question may simply be, Why is loving more difficult than hating? Or is it?

February 22: Kindness has something to do with time, a commodity which in this culture is always in short supply. But if we don't take time to be kind, on what will our lives really be spent. And to what end?

February 23: The climate of a home, an office, a room is made one person at a time. Waiting for someone else to make it a better, more pleasant place is to wait in vain. If you don't like the environment around you, change it.

February 24: Don't be afraid to smile at someone. Being out of character is sometimes good for all of us.

February 25: It takes one neighbor on every block to bring the rest of the block together. Do you have one? And if not, why aren't you it?

February 26: To be kind does not mean to smother someone; it means simply to attend to that person gently, caringly, thoughtfully. Smothering is simply one more form of control.

February 27: Kindness does not expect to be repaid. That is its real measure.

February 28: The Zen master teaches that one day Chao-chou fell down in the snow and called out, "Help me up! Help me up!" A monk came and lay down beside him. Then Chao-chou got up and went away. Point: To be kind does not require us to solve anything for others. It simply requires that, like God, we stay with them in their struggles until they are strong enough to get up and go their own way alone again.

March

PSALM 46:10

Be still and know that I am God.

It had been one of those weeks: back-to-back people, one meeting after another, deadlines unmet on every level, the calendar cops waiting around every corner. It was time to get back to center. It was time for space and quiet and a sensible reflection on exactly what was going on in life. A friend and I headed for the boat. On that boat everything in life took on perspective.

The lake lay still and gray in the early evening sun when I pushed out through the mouth of the marina. We headed the boat due north, toward Canada, and straight for the open water. We idled past the small fishing boats that sat frieze-like along the fringe of the bluffs above them and pushed beyond the mist that hung quietly over the water. Far in the west, the sunset blazed orange and ochre from one end of the sky to the other. And the silence, the emptiness, of the night made life human again.

Suddenly, the little boat began to rock and pitch, a lake's signal of disturbance before any disturbance is in sight. Then, out of nowhere, a roar ripped the water open behind us. Water washed in over the stern. The lake shuddered and rolled. Our small boat pitched and rocked helplessly in the water. Finally, while the larger boats *did circles around us, water skiers in tow, the booming started, one boom box on each boat, each playing something different, each loud and raucous and unintelligible. The sunset went to dust. The mist vanished in a swirl of wake. I turned around. The lake had filled with boaters with boom boxes. The silence shattered like broken glass. What, I wondered, had happened to us? Had contemplation disappeared and technology taken its place? Or had technology consumed to its peril one of the few remaining sanctuaries of humanity, those chancels that humanize humans and so make technology safe for human consumption? How is it possible to develop a contemplative heart in a world in chaos?*

March 1: The function of technology is to support the human endeavor, not to make it impossible. What science does not humanize it reduces to the inhumane. Marguerite de Valois said, "Science conducts us, step by step, through the whole range of creation, until we arrive, at length, at God."

March 2: When we allow technology to smother the values that nourish the human spirit, we have given over our souls to soullessness. We become efficient robots rather than reflective human beings.

March 3: Silence has become a rare and precious commodity in this world. But without it, how can we ever get to know ourselves?

March 4: "A science which does not bring us nearer to God is worthless," Simone Weil wrote. The purpose of science is to add possibility to the human condition. What we do with those possibilities measures the quality of our own souls.

March 5: Science is not neutral. Science is the question that confronts us with spiritual choices that mark the level of our human development. As Buckminster Fuller put it, "When I am working on a problem, I never think about beauty. I think only how to solve the problem. But when I have finished, if the solution is not beautiful, I know it is wrong."

March 6: When we find that we cannot balance contemplation and technology in our lives, technology must be controlled or we will give ourselves away to speed and noise and never even know that we have lost ourselves.

March 7: When life is going too fast to think about it, contemplation has given in to science. It is at that point, and that point only, that science becomes dangerous. Or we become wood. One or the other. An Arabic proverb teaches: It is good to know the truth, but it is better to speak of palm trees.

March 8: The contemplative asks of everything in life — this incident, this person, this pain, this beauty — What of God is in this thing for me? Not to ask that of everything is to forfeit the chance to be both human and spiritual.

March 9: A night without television is a night when the soul is let free. There is no substitute for the drama that goes on within the self.

March 10: It is always spiritual questions that undergird the life issues in which we find ourselves. Marriage, business, children, professions are all defined as if contemplation did not need to be a natural part of them. But no one needs contemplation more than the harried mother, the irritable father, the ambitious executive, the striving professional, the poor woman, the sick man. Then, in those situations, we need reflection, understanding, meaning, peace of soul more than ever. Contemplation is the missing quality of the beleaguered life.

March 11: Spiritual techniques and psychological quick fixes do not give substance to our lives. Only by going inside ourselves to clear out the debris of the heart rather than to concentrate on trying to control the environment and situations around us do we change the texture of life.

March 12: Contemplation leads us to see into the present with the eye of the soul so that we can see into the glimpse of heaven that each life carries within itself.

March 13: Contemplation, the willingness to see as God sees, perhaps does not change the difficulty, the boredom, the evil of a pernicious, an insidious situation. But it can change the texture of our own hearts, the quality of our own responses, the depth of our own understandings.

March 14: Contemplation has something to do with the ways in which we choose to grow. We can grow noisy, grow functional, grow efficient, and grow numb of heart, or we can grow into meaning, into humanity by taking the time to examine our own life in the light of the fullness of Life.

March 15: The making of interior space for the cultivation of the God-life is of the essence of contemplation. Interiority is the entering of the self to be with the God who leads us within, beyond, and out of ourselves to become the vessel of Divine Life which we are each meant to be.

March 16: Contemplation is not about going to church, though going to church ought certainly to nourish the contemplative life. Contemplation is about finding the God within, about making sacred space in a heart saturated with advertisements and promotions and jealousies and ambitions, so that the God whose spirit we breathe can come fully to life in us.

March 17: There is a danger in the contemplative life. The danger is that contemplation is often used to justify distance from the great questions of life.

March 18: Contemplation, for some, becomes an excuse to let the world go to rot. It is a sad use of the contemplative life and, at base, a bogus one. If contemplation is coming to see the world as God sees the world, then see it clearly we must. "Science without religion is lame," Albert Einstein wrote, and "religion without science is blind."

March 19: If contemplation means to become immersed in the mind of God, then we must come to think beyond our own small arenas.

March 20: If contemplation is taking on the heart of God in the heart of the world, then the contemplative, perhaps more than any other, weeps over the obliteration of the will of God in the heart of the universe.

March 21: Contemplation, the search for the sacred in the tumult of time, is not for its own sake. To be a contemplative is not to spend life in a spiritual jacuzzi designed to save humanity from the down and dirty parts of life. It is not an entrée into spiritual escapism.

March 22: Contemplation is immersion in the driving force of the universe, the effect of which is to fill us with the same force, the same care, the same mind, the same heart, the same will as that from which we draw.

March 23: Contemplation brings us to a state of dangerous openness. It is a change in consciousness. We begin to see beyond boundaries, beyond denominations, beyond doctrines, dogmas, and institutional self-interest straight into the face of a mothering God from whom all life comes.

March 24: To come to the awareness of the oneness of life is to regard all of it as sacred trust.

March 25: Contemplation is not ecstasy unlimited; it is enlightenment unbounded by parochialisms, chauvinisms, genderisms, classism. The breath of God, which the contemplative sets out to breathe, is the breath of the spirit of compassion. The true contemplative weeps with those who weep and cries out for those who have no voice.

March 26: Transformed from within, the contemplative becomes a new kind of presence in the world, signaling another way of being, seeing with new eyes and speaking with new voice the Word of God.

March 27: The true contemplative can never again be a complacent participant in an oppressive system. From contemplation comes not only the consciousness of universal connectedness of life but the courage to model it as well.

March 28: Contemplation breaks us open to ourselves. The fruit of contemplation is self-knowledge. "The nearer we draw to God," Abba Mateos said, "the more we see ourselves as sinners." We see ourselves as we really are, and knowing ourselves we cannot condemn the other.

March 29: Contemplation is not a private devotion; it is a way of life. It changes the way we think. It shapes the way we live. It challenges the way we talk and where we go and what we do. We do not "contemplate" or "not contemplate." We live the contemplative life that sees God in all things and treats all things as sacred.

March 30: The life question for the contemplative is a real one. Feodor Dostoevski put it simply but clearly: "Imagine that you are creating a fabric of human destiny with the object of making humanity happy in the end...but that it was essential and inevitable to torture to death only one tiny creature...and to found that edifice on its unavenged tears: would you consent to be the architect on those conditions? Tell me, and tell the truth!"

March 31: Just remember this: The cast-iron bathtub was first produced in 1870. The telephone went commercial in 1887. Just imagine: If you had been born in 1870 you could have spent seventeen years in the bathtub without being interrupted by the telephone. Now we know what happened to contemplation.

April

LUKE 12:49

I came to set fire to the earth,
and I wish it were already on fire!

I doubt that I will forget the situation for a long, long time. Correction: I hope that I will never forget the situation. After all, if and when I do, it may well say something about my own attitude toward life.

The woman I have in mind was eighty-one at the time of the conversation. She had just decided, I was told, to go with three other women about her own age on a train trip to San Francisco. I paused at the very thought of it. I was in my fifties, well-traveled, seasoned, but absolutely aghast at the thought of going by Amtrak all the way across the United States at any age, let alone at the age of eighty-one.

"How long are you going to be there?" I asked. "Oh, I think about three weeks," the old woman said. "After all," she went on, "I've never been there before, and I have no idea how long it will be before I go again." Here was a conversation stopper of major proportions. Again? Right. Again.

That, I decided then and there, was an icon I would hang on the wall of my mind forever entitled "Live till you die. Nothing else is worthy of life." There is so much life that is never lived because we lack the enthusiasm

*to live it. The problem is that I have seen apathy —
that deep-down, bone-weary lethargy that passes too often, I think, for calm — and I know that, though it is not
death, it is not life either. It may be false sophistication.
It may be depression. It may be ageism — at any age. But
it is not life.*

*I'm with Jesus: I prefer fire to smoke. And God knows
there is plenty of reason for fire in a world in which apathy has become both a social virtue and a contagious
disease.*

April 1: To go to a party without being willing to party is to ruin the night for everybody else. It takes enthusiasm to create enthusiasm.

April 2: Helen Keller wrote once, "Science may have found a cure for most evils; but it has found no remedy for the worst of them all — the apathy of human beings." And that in a world complacent about war, unconscious of sexism, blasé about hunger, unmoved by ageism, and disdainful of poverty. Helen Keller, no stranger to affliction, may have identified the greatest affliction of them all, a lack of enthusiasm for life.

April 3: It's so much easier to criticize life than it is to participate in it with an open mind, a willing spirit, and a joyful heart. Enthusiasm does not come with a barb and a sneer. Enthusiasm comes with a smile and with open arms.

April 4: There is no heavier weight in a group than apathy. When people refuse to take an interest in something, they condemn it to invisibility.

April 5: There is nothing in life worth doing that is not worth doing with enthusiasm. Anything else is simply a matter of going through the motions.

April 6: Clarence Day wrote once, "You can't sweep other people off their feet if you can't be swept off your own." To get others to care about what we care about, they have to see us care about it deeply. Have you cared about anything deeply lately? How would anybody know it?

April 7: The energy we bring to a thing determines our effectiveness in it. Nothing diminishes us more than our own lack of interest in life.

April 8: Passivity is not a sought-out virtue. If you're wondering why no one ever asks you to do something, ask yourself how many things you've shown any enthusiasm for lately.

April 9: To be without enthusiasm is to be without effectiveness. Marshmallow is not something that makes engines run.

April 10: Enthusiasm ought not be confused with hysteria. Enthusiasm is honest, positive response to a genuine issue. It has foundation, balance, and purpose. Hysteria is emotion that has, as the Irish say, "lost the run of itself." Or as William McFee puts it, "The world belongs to the enthusiast who keeps cool."

April 11: Showing an interest in life is a quality to be cultivated for the sake of our own mental health. Anything else leads inevitably to the damping of the soul.

April 12: To go through life without being deeply interested in something is an invitation to depression. After all, why go on if we haven't provided for ourselves something worth going on for?

April 13: Indifference is the enemy that lurks within us, waiting to smother us with our own smallness. The year in which I do not cultivate a new interest or feed an old one is a year of spiritual danger.

April 14: We restrain our own interests in order to make ourselves acceptable to everyone else and their interests. Too much of that and we run the risk, in the end, of winding up without a self.

April 15: Enthusiastic people make everybody around them feel alive. They give the rest of the world something to react against, at least. That in itself is a gift that takes the pulse of the rest of humanity.

April 16: Playwright Bertolt Brecht wrote: "Do not fear death so much, but rather the inadequate life." When we build no fires in our hearts, we live on ashes forever.

April 17: Enthusiasm for an idea, an event, a person, a plan is what keeps the universe turning. If nothing is worth doing, why do anything at all? We can simply sit down and rot in our own juices.

April 18: It isn't effort that kills the spirit; it is lack of effort that drains our energy. When the purpose is not worth the life, there is nothing that can substitute for the energy, the enthusiasm, that purpose brings.

April 19: "What makes life dreary is want of motive," George Eliot wrote. To keep going when there is no reason to go takes more effort than a person can sustain. Enthusiasm is the gift of motive.

April 20: Don't do a thing because someone tells you that you must. Do the thing because you know you must, because every beat of your heart tells you that you must. The energy, the enthusiasm we do not bring to a thing will in the end be what defeats us, not the thing itself.

April 21: "What hunger is in relation to food," Bertrand Russell wrote, "zest is in relation to life." Everyone yearns for something to live for, but the enthusiasm we develop as we go is key to finding it.

April 22: Life does not come to us for nothing. It can be bought only at the price of our own involvement. It takes an enthusiasm for beginnings to recognize life when we see it.

April 23: "He disliked emotion," John Buchan wrote, "not because he felt lightly, but because he felt deeply." Enthusiasm is not emotion without restraint. It is emotion without repression.

April 24: A lack of enthusiasm erodes the heart. People who cannot develop an interest in anything beyond themselves are people without a life. Being able to function is not enough. We need to be able to stretch ourselves beyond the mundane as well. Or why have heart, soul, mind, and body to begin with?

April 25: "The great art of life," Lord Byron wrote, "is sensation, to feel that we exist, even in pain." When we cease to feel, we cease to live. Enthusiasm is feeling for life, the awareness that in every event is the possibility of more life.

April 26: It is feeling that drives us, not reason. Einstein, Salk, Curie would never had made the discoveries they did without the enthusiasm they brought to their work. Whatever we do without enthusiasm will only be half done.

April 27: What we have no enthusiasm for, we can never learn from. What a pity. Enthusiasm is simply the willingness to try what we never tried before and find it wonderful.

April 28: Enthusiasm is the by-product of vision. Those who see a better world have a great taste for it.

April 29:   When we stop living before we stop breathing, we betray the very meaning of life. Enthusiasm is our obligation to the universe.

April 30:   Beware those who bring indifference into every conversation and every event they talk about. They carry within themselves the poison of life.

May

You are the light of the world.

Words are wonderful things. I have always loved them. They expose the human heart to the light of day; they protect in darkness what are the secrets of the soul. But I wonder sometimes if, however powerful the words, they can possibly have the impact of one picture.

Someday I will make a list of the photographs that have shaped my life. I know some of them without thinking: Nelson Mandela walking spry and determined out of a South African prison after twenty-six years in jail; Jackie Kennedy crawling over the back of a moving car in an attempt to get help for John Kennedy, her wounded husband, our bleeding president; a naked Vietnamese child aflame with American napalm on a quiet country road; the young father I never knew standing tall and gentle over my small self just before he died; an old nun on crutches baking bread in a large monastery kitchen; Pope John XXIII smiling in the midst of an institution not known for smiles; and one lone young man in a sea of faceless onlookers staring down a Chinese tank in the center of Tiananmen Square.

Those snapshots carry veins of meaning for me. They are all pictures of people facing life with every ounce *of strength within them. When the day is long and the project is failing, they say to me: Be strong. Stand firm. Go on. Don't quit. Be who you are and what you must be whatever the pressures against you. Be clear as glass always. Be it to the very end. Why? Because the scripture says, starkly telling, resounding for its simplicity: "You are the light of the world." What people see in you, they know to look for within themselves. What people see in you, they too may hope to extract from the depths of their own hearts.*

We are, each one of us, stones skipped across the waters of the universe. The ripples of our presence, whatever it is, good or bad, radiates forever. As you go, in other words, so goes the world. Now tell me again: What is it in life that you want someone else to correct?

May 1: Where we stand, and how steadfastly we stand there, what we see through to the end and how we do it, what we endure and embody, determine the character of our small portion of the world. That may be limited territory, yes, but it is all the world we have.

May 2: It is no small feat to turn global issues into personal ones: People are starving so I support the local soup kitchen. People are violent so I support handgun legislation. People are unemployed so I give them work. It's simple. The world is not out there. It is within six feet of me at all times.

May 3: "The salvation of humankind," Alexander Solzhenitsyn wrote, "lies only in making everything the concern of all." The problem is that we like to assume that everything needs to be solved "out there" when, in fact, it all needs to be solved within my own heart.

May 4: We pride ourselves on the fact that "we don't get involved" in things that are outside the local arena. But there is nothing in the world that isn't already deeply embedded there: poverty, hunger, pesticides, child abuse, discrimination, and political indifference are in every neighborhood, every institution. But there's no insurmountable problem, no unsolvable problem, until you and I think that none of them are our problems.

May 5: It's getting up every morning and doing what needs to be done that, in the end, measures the merit of a person.

May 6: It's not winning that matures us; it's staying where we need to be and doing it well that makes the difference between living well and living superficially.

May 7: It's so easy to assume that all the really important things in life are being done by someone else in some other part of the world. In the end, that leaves a great deal undone where we are.

May 8: "The path of duty lies in the thing that is nearby," the Chinese proverb says, "but we seek it in things far off." Getting so involved in the "big" things that we have no time to live life where we are is one of life's greater fallacies. It's called escapism.

May 9: "In dreams begin responsibility," William Butler Yeats wrote. The vernacular of that may not be poetic, but it is surely clear: Don't sit around wishing something would happen. Gather the people who can help you and see that it gets done.

May 10: All we can each do about anything is our small part. It is not immoral to have little to give, but it is an indecency to do less than we can. "She is poor indeed," Thomas Fuller says, "that can promise nothing."

May 11: Just being able to endure with equanimity what cannot be changed is its own kind of gift to those around us who are tempted to quit.

May 12: There are things in life that are more important than life. If not, then nothing will ever be better for those who come after us. The question is, What are they?

May 13: Life is not a free ticket to Disneyland. It requires commitment. If there is no one and nothing in life for which I feel responsible, for which I take responsibility, I haven't grown up yet. And time is running out.

May 14: The really hard thing about life is that it grinds inexorably on. And the really beautiful thing about life is that it grinds inexorably on. Life gives all of us a chance to begin over again and again. As long as we're willing to endure the weariness that comes with effort and the humiliation that comes with failure, there is time enough for everyone to know success.

May 15: "There is no duty we so much underrate," Robert Louis Stevenson wrote, "as the duty of being happy." We can get so dour about dailiness. But it is precisely when we allow ourselves to enjoy the routines of life that we find a happiness that can never elude us.

May 16: There is one thing that every one of us can bring to life, and that is the commitment to do our best to make it a better place when we leave it than it was when we came.

May 17: Doing what I can do is not the same as attempting to control everything that everybody else does. This does not help other people to live healthy lives, and, eventually, the frustration that comes when the world does not go as I had planned will destroy me too. Or as the wag put it: He was never happier than the day he resigned as general manager of the universe.

May 18: Everything that's wrong in the world is not because the world is essentially bad. It is because I do so little to show the world around me how to change it for the better.

May 19: Good things don't disappear. They simply cease to live in us.

May 20: We work hard at being responsible human beings for years: We take the political climate seriously. We work on civic projects. We model a life where everyone is welcome, everyone is valuable. We become active in civic affairs. But then we get tired of working for ideas that seem unpopular, out of reach, impossible. We decide to coast the rest of the way through life. That's exactly when we need to remember what generations before us understood so well. The Indians say: An arch never sleeps. Time to begin that thankless project one more time.

May 21: Robert Falcon Scott, who died exploring the North Pole, left a diary behind. It read: "Had we lived I should have had a tale to tell of the hardihood, endurance and courage of my companions which would have stirred the heart of every Englishman. These rough notes and our dead bodies must tell the tale." And, indeed, nothing could have spoken more clearly.

May 22: The question is, For what will you and I be remembered? For trying and quitting or for trying and missing? If life is going to be really holy, we need people who are more willing to bear honorable defeat than they are to live a life without honored purpose.

May 23: "Failure after long perseverance," George Eliot wrote, "is much grander than never to have a striving good enough to be called a failure."

May 24: Responsibility stretches life beyond the personal to the human. We were not born simply to stand around and breathe here. We were born to bring a gift into the world without which the world would be a poorer place.

May 25: It isn't escaping difficulty that makes us great, it's living through it, facing up to it, wrestling it to the ground of our souls.

May 26: What one snapshot will the world remember of you? For what human memory of greatness are you responsible in your little corner of the world?

May 27: "It is not your obligation to complete your work," the Talmud says, "but you are not at liberty to quit it." We come as part of the long chain of humanity, each one of us with another brick to lay in the edifice that is humanity. Stopping before we've done our part in building up the human race is to betray the entire chain.

May 28: Refusing to go away in the face of opposition may be the most revolutionary thing a person can do. "Brute force crushes many plants," D. H. Lawrence wrote. "Yet the plants rise again. The Pyramids will not last a moment compared with the daisy."

May 29: Even in the most extreme of circumstances, no one can really defeat us but ourselves. Or as Sir Winston Churchill told England in the face of a Europe at war: "Sure I am of this, that you have only to endure to conquer. You have only to persevere to save yourselves."

May 30: Endurance is what makes the difference between failure and success. The poet W. E. Henley wrote, "In the fell clutch of circumstance / I have not winced nor cried aloud: / Under the bludgeonings of chance / My head is bloody, but unbowed." Of course life bruises those who set out to make it better. But a few little bruises are no excuse for running away from what may be, for us, life's one great noble act.

May 31: The old couple had been married for years, and they were getting a bit forgetful about things so they decided that the way to meet their responsibilities was to write important things down. One night while they were reading the paper, the old man got up and started out to the kitchen. "Want anything while I'm up?" he asked. "Oh, yes, bring me some ice cream," said the old woman. "Don't forget to write it down before you go." "I can remember ice cream," he said. "But I want strawberries too," she said. "You better write this down." "I'm not that bad off, I can remember ice cream and strawberries," he replied. "Maybe," she answered, "but I want whipped cream on it too; so write it down." "Ridiculous," he muttered and disappeared into the kitchen. When he came back twenty minutes later, he was carrying a platter of bacon and eggs. "Now look what you've done. You didn't write it down," his wife said. "I knew you'd forget the toast." So much for rigid responsibility. In the end it's the thought that counts.

June

JEREMIAH 18:6

*Like clay in the hand
of the potter,
so are you in my hand.*

We know a great deal about trauma. We know, at least, that it happens to other people. Newspapers are full of the details: muggings, rapes, fires, murder attempts, wars and plagues and blights of all modes and manners. Compared to that kind of thing, we're inclined to think, the rest of us have led very benign and pedestrian lives with little to mark them and less about them to mark us. But that has not been my experience. I have yet to meet a human being who is not in some way still dealing with traumas, most of them garden-variety incidents, perhaps, but traumas nevertheless. Every one of us goes through some kind of personal pain of psychic wounding in life that changes us. It changes the way we look at the rest of the world; it changes the way we feel about ourselves. In fact, most of us go through many such experiences.

One of mine, definitely a shock of the lesser kind, stays with me still. It was the kind that most of us never forget but all of us are too embarrassed to discuss for want of its public legitimacy in the pantheon of disasters. I was ten years old, a transplant from another school and eager for insertion in the new one. But when acceptance came I was not available. The night before I was to be the angel who would lead the procession of first communicants to the altar

74

in a sweep of white satin and glory, my appendix heated to the bursting point and all my dreams came to a crashing end. While another girl made the grand entry in my place, I was being prepared for surgery amid a flurry of tense doctors and the protective presence of anxious parents. They all worried about my dying; I worried about having to live with such a loss. After that, I know, I ceased to assume that the great good promises of life could ever really be counted on to keep their appointments with fate. I also learned, however, that it isn't really necessary. When the hospital stay was over, Grandma came to visit, Mom got me a bird and Dad bought the bike. What we expect to have happen in life and what really happens are two different things, yes, but who's to say that what we planned was really better in the long run than what we got.

Everybody has a story of twists and turns along the way that shook their certainties about life. Each of them reshapes us, if only slightly, for the work of living. But they are not the tragedies of life; they are only its traumas. They break us open to reality. They give us faith in the dark and trust in the trying times. Trauma toughens us, seasons us, tempers us for the days when dull and drab could take us down unless we learn early that whatever happens, we can survive it laughing because, we someday discover, God has been in it all the way. In which case, whatever the pain, it is a very holy wound.

June 1: "If we had no winter," Anne Bradstreet wrote, "the spring would not be so pleasant." It is what we lose in life that teaches us to value what we have.

June 2: Life is a series of second chances, each of which gives us the opportunity to shape and re-shape life as we know it. When we do it thoughtfully and with open arms, it can be even better than we had hoped for on the days when life was bleak and unstable.

June 3: Character is what's left over after we have sunk to the depths of ourselves and reemerged to live again. Harriet Jacobs puts it this way: "Lives that flash in sunshine, and lives that are born in tears, receive their hue from circumstances."

June 4: Suffering is a part of life. Only those who think otherwise are doomed to be eternally unhappy. The others take suffering as the gateway to new life.

June 5: It is the wounds we carry that catapult us into possibility. It's when we're wounded that we live life most intensely. "A wounded deer leaps highest,"

Emily Dickinson wrote. When life stings most, leap we do. In fact, maybe nothing else really moves us nearly as well as the surprises of life that shock our system.

June 6: We have only one of two choices in the midst of trauma and woundedness: We can either go into decline or we can make up our minds to try again. The choice is ours. In the end, nothing can save us from ourselves but ourselves.

June 7: Everything we survive in life leads us to another level of growth, another experience of self-understanding. We spend our lives trying to understand the people and things around us when it is our own responses and reactions that may most need our attention. It's not so much what happens to us that is likely to level us; it's what we allow ourselves to think about it.

June 8: It's where we want to be that consumes us, but it is where we are that counts. Louisa May Alcott says that in order to live well we must be "resolved to take Fate by the throat and shake a living out of her."

June 9: To seek escape from suffering is to seek escape from life. Maybe it can be done but the shallowness such dearth implies is overwhelming for its paucity of soul, empathy, and compassion. Nothing teaches us more about the beauty of life than its periods of suffering.

June 10: "One does not die from pain," Warako Yamauchi writes, "unless one chooses to." Pain is the only proof we have that we are still alive and growing. It would be a pity to waste it.

June 11: God is not distant from suffering. God is in suffering, stretching us. Or as Aughey puts it: "God brings us into deep waters, not to drown us but to cleanse us."

June 12: Roberto Benigni in receiving the Academy Award for *Life Is Beautiful* thanked his parents for "giving him the greatest gift of all: poverty." The effort he needed to put into life to survive on his own made him what he is, in other words. It's something to think about when we dedicate ourselves to living a stress-free life.

June 13: It's not the life we have that matters; it's the life we make that counts.

June 14: The wounds of life are what make for the scar tissue of the soul. And scar tissue is always stronger than normal tissue.

June 15: "Life," Nathaniel Hawthorne wrote, "is made up of marble and mud." What Hawthorne neglected to say is that both of them are used by architects and artists alike.

June 16: Pain is the sign that something needs to be changed. Without trauma and woundedness we might never move off the spot we're in to the spot we should be.

June 17: When pain and suffering, humiliation and fear take us down into the deepest parts of the self, resurrection is only one thought away.

June 18: We all carry secret wounds somewhere. The thorn of the wound is what keeps us aware of the pain of others and the limits of our own egos. We may be invincible but we are not invulnerable. If anything can stop us from wounding another it is the memory of our own pain.

June 19: When we have finally turned the wounds of our souls into the stuff of our wisdom, we are valuable to someone else. Until then, we are no more than shells of a human being with little or nothing to teach the world.

June 20: Anaïs Nin writes: "We do not grow absolutely, chronologically. We grow sometimes in one dimension, and not in another, unevenly. We grow partially. We are relative. We are mature in one realm, childish in another." It is surely our childishness in one area that challenges our maturity in another. It is our maturity in one dimension that challenges our childishness in another. That's why we're always in internal conflict. One part of us is trying to outgrow the other.

June 21: From our anxieties about life come internal conflict, deep uncertainty, and psychological tensions. "Growing pains," your mother called it; "trauma," your psychologist calls it.

June 22: We don't create our destinies; we only shape them.

June 23: We can be positive about the future, knowing that we will get out of it what we put into it. Or we can be negative about the future, sure that having suffered once we are doomed forever. The positive approach trusts that tomorrow is full of possibility. The negative approach believes only in yesterday, a complete rejection of the God of the future.

June 24: Whatever it was that, in the course of our development, made us wary of the future also told us what we needed to do in the future if we were ever to get beyond the obstacles in ourselves. When we discover what it is we fear, for instance, we know what it is we need to face in life in order to be strong.

June 25: Life lies in taking all the pieces of our lives, considering what has been the function of each, and growing beyond them to the person we want to be now.

June 26: Whatever has marked us in our souls remains within us as a warning knell, not that the same thing will happen again but that we are not beyond it yet.

June 27: Deep suffering is nothing but a reservoir for deep joy. There is something out there waiting to fill it for us if we are only willing.

June 28: It is one thing to have been wounded. It is another thing to go through life licking our wound.

June 29: Whatever it is that wounds us simply shows us where it is that we have yet to grow.

June 30: Thank God for all the traumas you've had in life. They are the measure of your maturity.

July

LUKE 17:20–21

The Reign of God is within you.

She's small and frail and very old. On the cusp of ninety, in fact. They've had her dead now three times but she just keeps on going. Her mind is clear and she's steady on her feet, but those are not the things about her that fascinate me. It's something far more amazing than that.

I've known her for over forty years, and I have never seen her not smiling. Ever. That's forty-two years of smiles. She smiled at her students. She smiled at their parents. She smiled at the staff members with whom she worked. She smiled at strangers at the door. She smiled at us in days when smiling nuns were at a premium.

But there was something else about her that always charmed me a bit. I could never understand that smile. Was it vapid, empty, silly, naive? How can anyone smile for forty-two straight years? Unless, of course, there's something in them that's different, something about them that's unusual. Something about them that's holy.

As the years went by and I got to know her better, I figured out what it was about her that was different. She looked at life through a different filter than the rest of us. She didn't get old and cranky; she got older and more serene every day. It wasn't that she lived in a different world than the rest of us. It was just that she brought something to it that most of the rest of humankind seemed to be waiting for the world to bring to us.

It took psychologists years to explain to us that the thoughts we think have something to do with the quality of the life we live. But I didn't really need the instruction. I had been seeing it for years. And we see it yet. This woman thinks thoughts of peace and trust and care and acceptance. So she smiles. She never stops. The Reign of God is in that woman. She has a spirit no day can damp. She lives in the same world we do, but she clearly lives in it better than most.

P.S. She died shortly after this was written. The smile is gone now. Someone else will have to think the thoughts from here on in.

July 1: When I think dark thoughts, I act in dark ways. That's why depression is a social disease. It sours what it touches. To go through a day without thinking one good thought an hour is to starve the soul of life.

July 2: When I steep myself in negativism, I see joy nowhere and goodness seldom. The fact is that the way the world looks to me does not come from the outside of me; it comes from the inside of me.

July 3: It's not easy to put the best possible construction on the worst possible thing that happens in my day, but it is the most rewarding.

July 4: When we allow one bad incident to affect our whole day — our whole life, possibly — we allow "allness" to take over our lives. All the world we know, in other words, becomes discolored by one incident and we with it. Like one drop of ink in five gallons of water, it contaminates our entire lives. What a waste of the rest of that water.

July 5: Beware what you let yourself think about. For every negative issue in your life, be sure to balance it with a positive one: front-page crime in the morning, Rachmaninoff at night; anger at work, jokes at supper; disappointment in the family, social service on the weekend. That's not an exercise in denial; it's a contribution to world peace, a commitment to mental health.

July 6: The secret of a rich and happy life is to fill our souls with the kinds of ideas that make us more, and not less, human.

July 7: What you are, the world around you will be. But what you think is what you are.

July 8: The Chinese say, "To be uncertain is to be uncomfortable, but to be certain is to be ridiculous." To be too sure of anything is to make our own education impossible. You can never learn to think anything different that way.

July 9: There is no way to find out what I really think about anything until I keep quiet long enough to listen to what's really going on inside of me.

July 10: "There are no evil thoughts," Ayn Rand wrote, "except one: the refusal to think." Whatever truth we hold is amenable to review or it should not be held at all.

July 11: Every idea we have may not be "provable" in the scientific sense of the term, but if we "know" it, it controls our life. The question is, then, What purpose is that thought serving and is it making my world a happier, holier place, not only for me but for everyone around me as well? If not, it may be time to forget it.

July 12: Ideas rule the world. We must choose ours very carefully.

July 13: If we do not see ideas as the voice of God in us, how can we ever hope to know more of God in this world — and in ourselves?

July 14: To come to the end of life with a smile on the face has got to be an irrefutable sign of openness. To meet everything we see before us with delight is to live in such a way that we are always accessible to goodness.

July 15: There is no spiritual gain in closing off ideas in the name of rightness or goodness or traditionalism. "A closed mind," Edna Ferber wrote, "is a dying mind." As long as creation goes on creating, we can never come into its fullness by trying to stop its development.

July 16: What we bring to life is what we get out of life. Bring a sour attitude, get a sour response. Bring an open heart, get a heart full of happiness.

July 17: "Our life," Marcus Aurelius wrote, "is what our thoughts make it." For those who are their own god, the unexpected is a disaster. For those in whom life rages, the unexpected is God in disguise.

July 18: The more we look outside ourselves for the perfect world, the more we miss the world we were supposed to make for ourselves, the one inside us where resides everything we need to be happy.

July 19: Thoughts impel. The way we think about another person, the way we think about life, the way we think about ourselves is what will color the filter of our existence. If we want to change the way the world is for us, we will have to change the way we think about it.

July 20: The problem with the Reign of God is that it looks so different than the world we have learned to expect. In the Reign of God, people are basically good, life is rich with potential, happiness consists in having the basics of life and appreciating them, the purpose of life is to make the world a better place when we leave it than it was when we began. Instead, we learn early, people are not to be trusted, living is an arm-wrestling match, life is never happy unless you get more than you already have and the world is made for the person, not the person for the world. No wonder we don't smile as we go.

July 21: The way we look at the situation we're in determines the way we deal with it. If we believe that life is a series of opportunities, we recover from every blow and accept life with open arms. If we think that life is a series of disasters waiting to happen, life levels us and we crumple in the face of newness. "Thoughts are energy," Susan Taylor wrote. "And you can make your world or break your world by thinking."

July 22: I lost a leather wallet on a plane this week. The man to the right of me said, "You'll never see that again." The man to the left of me said, "There are a lot of honest people in the world. I bet you'll get a call." "Choose," I said to myself. I'll let you know what happens. In the meantime, I'm still smiling.

July 23: "An Englishman thinks seated; a Frenchman, standing; an American, pacing; an Irishman, afterward," says Austin O'Malley. And being Irish, I know that he has at least one of us right. But it might also be true that thinking about a thing after it happens — forming our impressions about it, drawing our conclusions about it, developing our ideas about it — is precisely what gives us the opportunity to experience it in the first place.

July 24: It isn't that people who think positive thoughts aren't being realistic. It's just that they are not being fatalistic. They take all of life one incident at a time instead of jumping to conclusions a year before the event.

July 25: When you think something negative about a thing, think again. It may not be what you're seeing that's important. It may be what you're missing that is the real truth.

July 26: Don't think that everything in life can be analyzed and evaluated and strategized. Some things simply need to be experienced. When you don't know what to think about a thing, smile at it.

July 27: It's when we take other people's ideas without adding anything of our own to them that we become one-dimensional people. It isn't that the goal is to contradict the rest of the world. It's simply that the goal is to know why we hold the ideas we do. "Think wrongly, if you please, but in all cases," Doris Lessing writes, "think for yourself." The Reign of God does not come vacuum-packed. It requires personal processing.

July 28: There's no such thing as serenity without thought. To accept the world around us without reflecting on it is not to be spiritually docile. It is to be intellectually comatose. The spiritual life is to be wrestled with, not swallowed whole.

July 29: When we see people who live in the center of chaos without themselves becoming chaotic, we have seen the Reign of God alive and smiling.

July 30: It takes a lot of listening to produce a lot of thinking. "Many a time I have wanted to stop talking and find out what I really believed," Walter Lippmann wrote. Don't be afraid to question your own beliefs. That's when God is most surely active in us. That's when we become spiritual adults.

July 31: There's not a thing in the world that can't be thought about differently. There's not a thing in the world that can't give us another way of looking at the world, if we are only open to it.

August

MATTHEW 14:13

*Jesus crossed the Sea of Galilee
to go someplace where he could be alone.*

*L*ong years ago, whenever I had an article or speech to write, I took a yellow pad, went into chapel, sat in my pew, stared into space, and began to write. To this day, I never go into chapel without a small notebook and pen. I never know what's going to go racing through my mind when things are still and orderly. I always thought of it as a very normal thing to do. I have begun to notice of late, however, that there is no run on yellow pads in the foyer outside of chapel. Most of those who come in carrying anything at all come in carrying books. I like this Benedictine community, and I find them holy. Whatever had happened to me that I come in carrying pen and paper? Is there something wrong with my spirituality? It became a very serious question.

Then one day I figured it out. Chapel is where I go to sink down into silence, to be in solitude whatever the size of the crowd, to think from the inside out instead of from the outside in. Silence and solitude, I discovered, were breeding grounds for ideas. Why? Because there is one place that is never silent. There is one place in which thought rages. And that place is in the silence that is inside the self. Until we go into silence, we have nothing *to say except what we hear around us, nothing to think except what has already been thought by somebody else. Until we go into silence, we may really know very little about ourselves.*

Silence is the sanctuary of the soul. Solitude is its bridge.

August 1: Pity people who can't stand to be alone. It means they have nothing worth working on inside themselves.

August 2: Silence is conversion's port of entry. It holds the layers of the soul. At the first layer is the public self with all its resentments and longings for acclaim. At the second layer is the self, with all its dreams and hopes. At the unfathomable center of the soul is the awareness of who I really am and who I could be if I ever attended to the deep running currents in me. Only in silence can I hear these whispered calls.

August 3: Silence is the sabbath of the soul. It enables us to rest from the noise and pace around us and think of softer things: a Mozart concerto, van Gogh's *Reaper,* the remnants of a long-lost poem.

August 4: In my town, people buy sandwiches at the deli and then go to the public dock or the end of the peninsula during their lunch hour. They sit in their cars, listen to the ducks, watch the flowing water, and let the world go by. They bring the self to the self. How unusual.

August 5: People say that there is no way to get the silence we need in this busy world without moving to a mountain cabin four times a year alone. Not true. We can make a zone of silence around us. We can do woodworking or pottery or photography or music. We can do something which takes us into that space where only we can go. And there with the chords and the buzz of the saw and the splash of the developing pans we can find ourselves and the God we seek.

August 6: There are two kinds of silence: one is bitter silence; the other is sweet silence. Bitter silence is the quiet that freezes people out. Sweet silence is the quiet that takes us inside ourselves so that we can come out later softer and humbler than before.

August 7: Scripture is very clear: God is not in the noise around us. God is in the whisper of the breeze. It takes concentration to hear God, in other words. The things we mistake for God, noisy, consuming, and encompassing as they may seem at first, will in the end have nothing new to say to us about ourselves, about life, about meaning. Only in silence does God say those things.

August 8: "One of the greatest necessities in America," Carl Sandburg wrote, "is to discover creative solitude." The solitude that cuts us off from others in order to avoid them is a sick, sick solitude. The solitude that enables us to refresh ourselves in such a way that we can go back among people more open than ever before is the solitude that is "re-creative."

August 9: There is a difference between silence and emptiness. Silence is a very busy thing. It opens us to the exploration of the self. Emptiness is the vacuum we find when something is missing from our lives and needs to be replaced.

August 10: We love crowds and noise and fanfare and fullness in this country. We want everything to be big and loud, the bigger and louder the better. "Silence is un-American," Erica Jong says. Maybe that's why we are such an unreflective society. We do what works in life, not necessarily what enhances life.

August 11: We give courses in this country on how to listen. It's a good idea because there is such a thing as listening with the other person in mind. At the same time, you have to wonder how many courses we'd need if we just sat and let someone else talk once a day. Without interrupting, without arguing the point, without neglecting to ask genuine questions about what the other person wants to talk about.

August 12: Silence is what enables us to be filled up with something besides ourselves.

August 13: Someday try doing nothing but sitting in an empty room and listening to what is playing on the tapes inside your head. Take a few notes. Now answer the question: What is really going on inside yourself?

August 14: Jesus wasn't running away from people. He was trying to get himself back after days of pouring himself out for others. Mothers could benefit from the example. And CEOs. And psychologists. And probably you.

August 15: "You can live a lifetime," Beryl Markham wrote, "and, at the end of it, know more about other people than you know about yourself." The question is why the hard work of self-knowledge, self-criticism frightens us so much.

August 16: People who have never spent a day in silence — who have to have the radio on or the TV blaring — are very lonely people who have yet to make peace with themselves.

August 17: If you want to think, you have to stop talking long enough to know what you thought.

August 18: They say that extroverts need to talk in order to think and that introverts talk only after they have thought a thing out. Maybe, but the interesting thing is when extroverts don't say what they're thinking and introverts do. Then we have conversation.

August 19: We are all full of the riches of a lifetime — the experiences we've had and the wisdom that has come from them; the dreams we've had and the things that obstructed them; the hurts we've had and the things that cured them. "I was never less alone," Edward Gibbon wrote, "than when I was by myself." What is important is that we give ourselves time to think all those things through. Then the rest of life will be richer.

August 20: Coming to understand ourselves takes a lot of silence. Maybe that is why so few do.

August 21: A day of silence is a new experience for many of us in this wired world of ours. How sad. That means that we are hardly ever just where we are anymore. We live always with a foot in two worlds: where I really am now and where my stimulation is coming from outside myself. Who am I now? is the kind of question that gets easily lost in an environment like that.

August 22: Silence is a calming thing. It hurries us nowhere and leaves us only with ourselves. There's the question: Is that good company for you yet or not?

August 23: We have in the silence of ourselves only what we ourselves have put there. The challenge of every noisy hour is to fill our thoughts with beauty and good.

August 24: Silence is what enables us to discover our questions as well as our answers. Otherwise we are doomed to drown out the very best in ourselves. No wonder we never get anywhere in life. We never listen to the thoughts in us that would take us there. Then at the end of life we say, "I always wanted to . . . and I should have listened to that urge." What is more pathetic than the unfinished life?

August 25: To learn the fruits of silence it is necessary to be silent.

August 26: If we really want to know who and what we are, the only way to do it is to listen to ourselves in silence. It can leave us with an agenda for a lifetime. It can also take away the stories we spin to ourselves about why we really do what we do.

August 27: Learning to be alone is the best way to learn silence. Then we have only ourselves for company and a chance to find out if that is good company or not.

August 28: When we are alone, in silence, we discover what it is that we really want to do, what it is that we're really afraid of, what it is that speaks of God in us.

August 29: Where is God? If God is in creation, then the answer must be that God is in the center of the self. Where else? How long has it been since I was there?

August 30: Solitude and silence are those places where the creative fountains flow. To be without these two dimensions of the self is to doom myself to the role of only a copy artist forever because, never able to hear the new things within myself, I can only repeat everybody else.

August 31: A policeman pulled a car over and told the driver he had won $5,000 in the seat belt competition just by being the five thousandth person to drive over the traffic counter wearing one. "What are you going to do with the money?" asked the policeman. "Well, I guess I'm going to get a driver's license," he answered. "Oh, don't listen to him," said a woman in the passenger seat, "He's a smart aleck when he's drunk." Then the guy in the back seat said, "I knew we wouldn't get far in a stolen car." At that moment there was a knock from the trunk and a voice said, "Are we over the border yet?" As I was saying about silence. . . .

September

PSALM 135:13

God gave their land as a birthright,
a birthright to God's people Israel.

*E*verybody gets a birthright. Most of us either don't recognize it or don't want it. And that makes all the difference.

I had a cousin who didn't like the brown eyes he'd been given. He wanted blue eyes like everyone else in his mother's family. Poor boy. He never did realize that being different from the rest of us was his opportunity to be himself, so he grew up feeling outcast rather than unique.

I myself lost a great music teacher when I was just coming into my own on the piano... and wound up becoming a writer instead.

My father was a small man who wanted to be a tall man — and because of his slight build ended up getting a draft deferment because he was the only man on the job who could do the final welds in the nose cones of LSTs, the landing craft that took an army ashore on Normandy Beach.

And the Chinese tell the story of a poor peasant farmer who had only one horse. One day, someone left the corral gate ajar, and the horse escaped into the mountains. Everyone in the valley commiserated with the old man for his loss. But the old farmer simply said, "Good event, bad event. Who knows?"

At the end of the summer, lo and behold, the lost horse came galloping down the mountain side, right into the corral, leading a herd of wild horses. Everyone in the valley rejoiced with the farmer over his newly found wealth. But the farmer said, "Good event, bad event. Who knows?"

That year, in the course of the harvest, one of the wild horses threw the farmer's only son and crippled him for life. Everyone in the valley grieved for the farmer whose son could no longer do the harvesting for him. But the old farmer simply said, "Good event, bad event. Who knows?"

Finally, the emperor sent his Master of the Guard into every village of the realm to enlist young men for the army. The Master took every man from every farm in the area — except for the farmer's crippled son. Everyone in the valley mourned for the loss of their children and rejoiced at the good fortune of the poor farmer, the only one of them who still had a son left to oversee his property. But the old farmer only said, "Good event, bad event. Who knows?"

The question is, what have you done with your birthright? The truth is that a birthright is simply what we make of it. Good event, bad event. Who knows?

September 1: Life is a series of circumstances, all of which lead to the fulfillment of the self. The fact that we resist or reject so many of them only slows the process.

September 2: All the elements of life conspire to make us great. The only thing we need to do is to embrace them. Instead, we spend so much energy bemoaning what we aren't instead of learning to love what we are.

September 3: Life is never lived in a straight line. We pitch and toss, revolve and reverse until the inside of us finally squares with the outside of us. Then we discover what we have been looking for all the time and couldn't find because it was within us.

September 4: The Zen master says: "If Enlightenment is not where you are standing, where will you look?"

September 5: Life is not handed to us whole. All we get of it is the pieces. The shaping of it is up to us. And it is a slow, slow process.

September 6: The trouble with getting older is that you discover what you missed along the way. The beauty of getting older is that you discover that you haven't missed anything at all. You just failed to value it.

September 7: Life is a complex of past experiences, future opportunities, and present options. It is the past we try to forget, and it is the future that we strive for. But it is the present, where experience and opportunity come together, that we are most inclined to miss.

September 8: When we find ourselves living largely either in the past or in the future, we know that life has gone askew. Then it's time to make the best of where we are if we want anything better to happen as time goes by.

September 9: "History moves in contradictory waves," Lois Beck wrote, "not in straight lines." As happens with pebbles in water, it is the push and pull of the undercurrent of our lives that smooth us out and wear us down to our real selves.

September 10: The birthright — what we really are and are meant to be — is at the base of all our strivings. Happiness lies, then, in giving ourselves over to the best in our most basic selves. That's why pushing children into the most highly paid vocations does not necessarily lead to their most highly satisfied selves.

September 11: When God gives us life, God gives us everything we need to sustain it. The components may look strange at the outset, but hindsight is a wonderful optic. The trick is to trust it before you can see it.

September 12: Don't give up on life before life gives up on you.

September 13: Every stage of life is another step toward its fulfillment. To cling to any of them is to arrest the development of all of them. The time for moving on is always now. As Charlotte Bernard wrote, "I cannot sing the old songs, / Or dream those dreams again."

September 14: Gretel Ehrlich wrote, "History is a story that changes and has accidents and recovers with scars." We all bear the scars of the past, true. Scars simply prove we were there.

September 15: Not all scars are ugly. Scars speak, too, of survival and learning and wisdom and hope. In fact, life without scars may be no life at all.

September 16: The past does not predict the future, but it often explains it. So much of what we do in life comes from what we were expected to do or wanted to escape. Learning to appreciate the best of the present is the only antidote.

September 17: My birthright is born again every day in me. It is those parts of myself that no one can take away from me and that are developing in me yet.

September 18: God gives us the land of ourselves to plant and grow, to develop and enjoy, to tend and complete. It is not what life has been for us in the past that counts; it is what we are harvesting from it now that is really important.

September 19: We get trapped in what we have been and bog down there. Ridiculed as a child, I still feel ridiculous. Rejected as a child, I still feel unaccepted. But Mary Antin writes, "It is not that I belong to the past but that the past belongs to me." It's the character to turn ridicule and rejection into courage that counts.

September 20: Everyone is given something to develop — a mind, a child, a talent, a piece of land, an idea. When we're not developing whatever it is, we are not developing ourselves. Then the birthright goes to dust.

September 21: "Sometimes a person has to go back, really back," Paule Marshall wrote, "to have a sense, an understanding of all that's gone to make them ...before they can go forward." When we get stuck in the past, we forget that we are obliterating the present. It's not what happened yesterday that matters. It's what we do today that makes the difference in the self.

September 22: A lot of people go to the best schools, have the best connections, make the best career moves — and are never heard from again. Or as the German proverb says, "Noble and common blood is of the same color."

September 23: If the present of some people is made up of the barely survivable, someone is responsible. And it's not God.

September 24: Hope is made of discontent. What drives birthright is hope.

September 25: When people are in dire straits, situations not of their own making, hope comes to make them discontented. It is that sacred discontent that brings the birthright to fulfillment.

September 26: The birthright is given to be satisfied now, as Canaan was given to Israel here, not in the next world.

September 27: When we tell people to offer up the destruction of themselves until the next world, we mock God in this world.

September 28: Birthright is the raw material of determination.

September 29: Wherever you've come from, whatever you've come through, are the makings of you. Celebrate them.

September 30: "Can anyone in here name something of importance that did not exist fifty years ago but does now?" the teacher asked the class. And a little girl shouted out from the back of the class, "Me!" Now that's birthright.

October

Ezekiel 37:4–5

*Dry bones, listen to what God is saying to you,
"I, the God of life will put breath in you,
and once again you will live."*

I was one of those people who considered parents a biological nicety but grandmothers a remnant of the divine. Mine was particularly divine. Grandma had hammer toes. She also had cancer. She died from the cancer but she worked on the hammer toes to the very end. "As soon as I can get these shoes on again, I can go round and visit everyone who's been so nice to me," she told me as she sat on the side of her bed and tried to stretch the leather of her big, black shoes to accommodate the ugly, bony, overlapping toes. The attitude burned itself into my soul. She certainly knew she had cancer in days when people didn't even whisper the word. But she also knew that she couldn't do a thing about the cancer. The hammer toes she thought she could do something about. And so with a kind of steely inner strength, she concentrated on the toes, not the cancer.

You can call it denial if you like — that would, of course, be the conclusion of the sophisticates — or you can call it serenity. The point is that the choice is clear: we can live in despair over a reality that we cannot do anything about, or we can attend to our little piece of it in hope. To this day, when the family remem-

bers that Grandma died from cancer, I sit there and think to myself, "Ah, yes, but she knew how to live with hammer toes."

It's always a toss-up: despair or serenity. Choose.

124

October 1: It isn't what we lose that will destroy our peace of mind. It is the serenity we fail to cultivate in our hearts when life is good that stands to take us down when life is difficult.

October 2: Serenity comes from accepting what is, shaping for the better whatever can be changed, and in the meantime refusing to spend the greater part of life wrestling with the inconsequential.

October 3: We waste too much time, too much nervous energy attempting to control what is too minor to bother trying to control. We fuss about a child's haircut, a spouse's eating habits, a neighbor's dog, an office mate's disorderly desktop and fail to worry about the relationships that underlie them all. No wonder we're upset most of the time.

October 4: There is an inner joy that far surpasses the joy that comes from externals. A new car will keep me in a good mood until the first scratch. The kind of joy that comes with going at life gently will last forever.

October 5: Joy is the ability to go on believing that life is good even when it definitely is not. Or as Erma

Bombeck put it: If life is a bowl of cherries, what am I doing in the pits?

October 6: Living in the present, doing what can be done now to make this particular moment a good one, is one of life's greatest lessons. "When we yield to discouragement," St. Thérèse of Lisieux wrote, "it is usually because we give too much thought to the past and to the future."

October 7: Anybody can do anything to make life around us miserable. No one can do anything to make life inside of us miserable — except us, of course.

October 8: The trouble with the way we go about life is that we usually try to take on too much of it at once. Is this present moment a good one for you? Then why are you so riled up about ones yet to come? Enjoy.

October 9: Despair is what we do when we give up on the Living God. Or when we think that we are God — and have failed.

October 10: "To eat bread without hope," Pearl Buck wrote, "is still slowly to starve to death." Every minute of life is the beginning of the next one. It's not enough simply to accept this one. We must do whatever we can to make the next one even better. To languish in the present without building for the future is to die from lack of growth.

October 11: To believe that life can be better than it is makes living a godly act. We are not here to consume life. We are here to create it for those who come after us.

October 12: We must not confuse hope and desire. Hope drives us to believe that the future will be as good to us as the past has been. Desire teaches us that no amount of anything is ever sufficient. It's hope we must cultivate. Otherwise no matter what we have, it will never be enough for us.

October 13: "Hope is the poor person's bread," George Herbert wrote. Hope sustains us through the dregs of despair. It is the voice in the heart that tells us that God meant us for good and will not permit bad to drown us in the ocean of life.

October 14: "Birds sing after a storm," Rose Kennedy told a reporter who wondered how she could keep going on after suffering so much family tragedy. "Why shouldn't people feel as free to delight in whatever remains to them?" Mourning what we have lost in life only obscures the beauty of what remains.

October 15: Everyone is struck down by something in life. It is the detour that determines the definition of the journey. We can lose our way then and there, stay stuck in unfamiliar territory, stall and give up. Or we can take the new direction confident that in the end we will end up exactly where we were meant to be whether we can see how that is possible right now or not.

October 16: Serenity and joy are not the same things. Joy is the capacity to respond to good. Serenity is the capacity to trust the present, however circuitous it seems right now. They're both important in life, of course, but serenity takes us further than joy does. Joy is the hallmark of the meaning of the moment. Serenity is the virtue of the long haul.

October 17: It's when we think we cannot bear another moment that serenity takes over to remind us that the present moment is simply one moment on a way that is long and surprising and beautiful.

October 18: "You won't find this year's birds in last year's nests," someone once wrote. Hope is what takes us beyond the present. Otherwise we would never grow another inch of soul.

October 19: "There never was night that had no morn," Dinah Craik wrote. What else can possibly get us through all the nights of our lives in better spirit than the awareness that we have survived everything else in life and been the better for it.

October 20: Anything that happens to us is simply one more point along the way meant to teach us one more thing about ourselves, about God, about life. God did not create us to destroy us wantonly.

October 21: Life is the living of one dawn after another until we get it right.

October 22: "The unendurable," Djuna Barnes wrote, "is the beginning of the curve of joy." Point: When things get bad enough, we'll do something about them. Everything else in life is simply the habit of worry.

October 23: To survive the social changes in which they operate, economists tell us that companies must reinvent themselves at all times. And so must we. It's when we decide to stay at the point to which we have come in life — socially, politically, economically, theologically — that life ends for us. Then we can only resist the present and grieve the past. Then we sin against the virtue of hope.

October 24: The Spanish proverb teaches: "God is always opening God's hand." What looks at first like disaster may actually turn out to be the gift of your life. But you must open your own hand to receive it.

October 25: "Hope is an echo," the poet Carl Sandburg wrote. "Hope ties itself yonder, yonder." Hope is what calls us beyond the present. It encourages us to try the unfamiliar, to accept the unacceptable, to see beyond darkness. It fastens our eyes on the future and makes the present possible.

October 26: Observe carefully what it is that throws you into paroxysms of despair. They are clues to the depth, the shallowness, of your soul.

October 27: "I'll have to, as you say, take a stand, do something toward shaking up that system," Paule Marshall admitted. "Despair...is too easy an out." How we love to give up on what we refuse to do something about. That makes it look as if the situation is the problem, when as a matter of fact, it is we who are lacking the courage, the commitment to change a thing.

October 28: Despair has a lot to teach us: It is in despair that we come to realize that time does not change things; people do.

October 29: For those of you who have been wondering what happened (see July 22): I lost a wallet, a business card holder, and a cell phone on three different flights in July. Well, I got all of them back from three different cities at three different times. Some people are in despair about the level of American morality. Not I. (I do despair a little about my flakiness, however.)

October 30: "How lovely is the sun after rain," the Jewish proverb teaches, "and how lovely is laughter after sorrow." It's what we lose that teaches us to suck all the juices out of every other moment in life.

October 31: The preacher was a rigid Temperance man in a loose and lively congregation. "If I had a cask of wine," he ranted, "I would throw it in the river." "If I had a keg of beer," he raved, "I would throw it in the river." "If I had a barrel of whiskey," he roared, "I would throw it in the river!" So at the end of the sermon, the organist got up and announced to the weary crowd, "We will now all sing hymn number 353: 'Let Us Gather at the River in the Morning.'" (See what I mean? Hope springs eternal....)

November

MATTHEW 1:15

*It is not what goes into the mouth that defiles;
it is what comes out of the mouth that defiles.*

I long ago learned that sin is not always what meets the eye. I remember the lesson well.

My father had been out of work — on strike — for weeks. It was shortly after the war, and the unions were pressing for higher wages and better benefits after a long period of hard work and personal sacrifice. I was very small but very aware that no work meant no money. I was worried about us as a family — How would we live if my father had no job? — and my mother was worried about my worrying. So one night, after another day of union violence, my father scooped me up out of my bed and carried me, blanket trailing, to the windows over-looking the main street of the little steel town where we lived. Then he made me tell him what I saw across the street. "A grocery store," I said. And what did I see in the front of the store, he wanted to know. "Windows," I said. "Right, Jo," my dad said, "and as long as there are windows on grocery stores, you and your mother will eat." I was horrified. "Daddy," I said, "You wouldn't break that window and steal things, would you?" After all, what would Sister say at school if she ever heard anyone say such a thing. I felt his arms tighten around me. "Honey," my father said, "when people have nothing to eat, it is not a sin for them to steal food."

In the second situation, the people down the street got divorced after years of quarreling and night after night of violence. In an age when divorce was unheard of anywhere, I was horrified then too. Wasn't divorce a sin? I asked. "Joan," my mother said, "it's far more sinful for those people to go on destroying one another and their children than it is for them to admit that they need to start over again for all their sakes."

Sin, I learned clearly, had more to do with how it affects our humanity and the lives of other people than it does with simply breaking the rules. It was a life lesson of awesome proportions. Being perfect is not always perfect at all. And sometimes keeping the rules, I came to understand, can be more sinful than breaking them.

November 1: "If you want to be properly sinful," the wag wrote, "it is not necessary to break the law. Just keep it to perfection." It is people who refuse compassion on the grounds of law that break the heart of God.

November 2: We spend a lot of time worrying about "sins of commission" — about the things we've done in life — and almost none worrying about "sins of omission" — about the things we've failed to do. And so, as a result, we have neglected children, social agencies that go begging for volunteers, justice issues ignored because it's not my problem. But strangely enough, I am the only solution.

November 3: We remember the times we scolded the children too harshly, but we forget when we took their goodness for granted and neglected to hug them. We worry about the lies we've told as we've gone through life, but we worry not a bit about the times we stood silent in the face of disapproval and failed to say a saving truth. We think about stealing, but we don't think that failing to give when we could give is also a sin. Sin is as much an attitude of mind as it is a body of behaviors.

November 4: Sin and evil are not the same thing. Sin has something to do with failing to be the best of what we are trying to be. Evil is malice unleashed against another with intent to do harm. Sin is in the air we breathe. It goes with growing. Evil has the smell of sulphur to it.

November 5: "All sins," Simone Weil wrote, "are attempts to fill voids." When something important — love, dignity, respect — is missing in life, we find something to replace it. Young people find the gangs that will include them. Adults find the drugs that will numb them. When I find myself grappling with any kind of excess, the question must be, For what emptiness in me am I trying to compensate?

November 6: Jesus knew the difference between doing something wrongful out of weakness and doing something dishonorable in order to harm another. That has to be the reason why he forgave the woman taken in adultery and condemned the men who intended to stone her.

November 7: There is, in everyone, the seed of greatness. To fail to grow to full stature morally is the greatest sin against the flowering of the self.

November 8: The major moral question has got to be why Jesus showed special love to sinners. Surely the answer must be that each of them had the virtue to admit their need for mercy. Most of the rest of us insist on defending our actions and arguing our essential correctness.

November 9: Getting to be perfect can be perfectly boring. It means that there is nothing else to learn in life.

November 10: The world is in the state it's in because there are things in me that need changing. When I begin to take responsibility for the character of the little world in which I live, the world will become a holier place to be for everyone.

November 11: Be at least as afraid of the kind of virtue that gives us the right to condemn everyone else as you are of a few private sins. Arrogance commits us to a community of one. There is nothing to be gained there.

November 12: Our sins may be the only thing that generates in us a compassion for the rest of the human race who, like us, have floundered from one life challenge to another.

November 13: To have nothing whatsoever to commend us to the world but our virtues is sure proof that we have not lived through enough yet to deserve the honor we seek.

November 14: Good can always come out of evil. But evil is no way to achieve good. Stooping to the level of the inhuman to do good does nothing to humanize the world.

November 15: Don't confuse weakness with sin. Most of us struggle with something we never quite conquer. It is precisely that struggle that can become the stuff of compassion for others.

November 16: Rationalization is a clever way of trying to talk ourselves out of what we know down deep should never have happened.

November 17: The time we spend worrying about not being perfect may be exactly what keeps us from doing good. If we wait till we're perfect in anything to do it, we will do very little in life.

November 18: Sin changes with age. In youth it is born out of impulse; in later years it is based in calculation. The first stage requires the ability to discriminate and the development of control. It's a period of experimentation that can end in wisdom. But at a later stage, when we have really come to "know good from evil," sin requires that we review the entire value system that drives us. Something has gone seriously awry. And in the end it is not just what our sin does to other people that counts; it is what sin does to us that matters deeply as well.

November 19: It's one thing to be about the business of growing up. It's another to grow up with a great gaping vacuum in the soul. Then it's time to take stock, to wonder what it is in life we're missing which what is beneath us even to contemplate is meant to satisfy.

November 20: Sin does as much to destroy us from the inside as it does to destroy the world around us. It means that we become less than we really want to be.

November 21: "He who condemns sin becomes part of it, espouses it," Georges Bernanos says in the spiritual classic *The Diary of a Country Priest*. To take upon ourselves the right to condemn the sinner is a sin. It puts us in the place of God. And that sin is greatest of them all.

November 22: When people steal and lie and wallow in excesses, bask in sloth and feed their lusts, we call it sin. When corporations do it we call it good business and success, the art of the deal, and Third World wage scales. Interesting, isn't it?

November 23: Piers Paul Reed said, "Sins become more subtle as you grow older: you commit sins of despair rather than lust." But God, who never gives up on us, wants us to make sure that we never give up on ourselves either.

November 24: There are worse things than emotional immaturity. There is such a thing as dearth of soul that comes with trying to find the fullness of life outside ourselves rather than by developing the fullness of life within us.

November 25: The value of sin is to learn forgiveness: how to get it and how to give it as well.

November 26: There are some things that can be learned only by sin. The history of sainthood is a history of sin: Teresa of Avila, Ignatius of Loyola, Charles de Foucauld all struggled their way to God as we do. Only when, like them, we discover the depths of our own neediness can we begin to discover our strengths and God's mercy.

November 27: People who have never faced their own sins are people who have yet to know themselves. But without self-knowledge, real spiritual development is impossible. Then, though we may be religious, we have yet to be spiritual.

November 28: Annie Dillard tells a story about a tribesman who said to the missionary, "If I did not know about God and sin, would I go to hell?" And the priest said to the tribesman, "Oh, no, if you didn't know about God and sin, God would not send you to hell." "Then why," the tribesman said, "did you tell me?"

November 29: The important thing to remember is, as Igor Stravinsky says, that "sin cannot be undone, only forgiven." What we do to ourselves or others stays in the soul like dust in the air. We cannot undo it. We can only begin again. For that reason, God has no memory.

November 30: "What God gave Adam," Elie Wiesel said, "was not forgiveness from sin. What God gave Adam was the right to begin again."

December

Genesis 1:31

*God saw all God had made,
and indeed it was very good.
Evening came and morning came:
the sixth day.*

The town in which I spent a large part of my early childhood years was the product of a wartime world. Clumps of square brick buildings, spectacular only for the depth of their drabness, clung to the perimeter of the steel company that gave rise to their existence. The place had grown up to fuel wartime industries and then, later, survived on the postwar economic thirst for creature comforts delayed: for refrigerators, for cars, for consumer goods denied while the war machine raged on. It was a town where people got up, went to the shops, came home to sleep and eat, and went back to the shops again the next day. It was a dour place.

Coal dirt belched from the chimneys of the large corrugated shop segments day and night. House paints, whatever their original colors, turned an inevitable uniform gray. Coal dust thickened every window pane. Every tiny sweet pea in every tiny window box died under the weight of the ash. Every flake of snow turned dark before it touched the ground. The streets flowed into sidewalks, the sidewalks into buildings. It was a cement jungle of smothering proportions.

My mother wanted out of there. She was tired, she said, of stretching curtains every week. She wanted to live "like a human being." The question in my young mind as she said it over and over again was, What did that mean and where did a person have to go to get it? And then I found out.

It was our second day in Erie, Pennsylvania. I was about ten years old. "Momma," I said, "this is the place where I want to live." My mother smiled a little. "And how can you be so sure of that so soon, Joan?" she said. "You've hardly seen the place." My mother was a practical woman. She didn't do things without "a good reason." "Because," I said back, sure of the logic of my argument, "there are trees on every street here." And indeed there were. Trees and thick bushes in big yards and wild grasses in open lots and live flowers everywhere. The place vibrated life.

I was sure then that I was correct in my criteria, and I'm even more sure of it now. The truth is that life is not only about living. Life is also, purely and simply, about life, about the holiness of creation, about God's love incarnate in the world around us. And, interestingly enough, I realize more and more every year, it is the spark of the divine in life that Christmas is meant to celebrate. It is fragile life, holy life, that Christmas hallows, that Christmas calls us to recognize, that Christmas reminds us to bow down before as we go.

How is it that we have lost our capacity to see the creator in creation? Is it possible that those who cannot see the divine in the created world have missed Jesus also? Is it possible that those who miss the humanity of Jesus miss the holiness of the rest of creation as a result? Merry Christmas. Celebrate life.

December 1: To understand Christmas is to come face-to-face with the incarnation. The very notion that God imbued creation with divinity makes everything we see sacred, every step we take a pilgrimage to the divine.

December 2: The Spanish writer José Ortega y Gasset wrote, "I am I plus my surroundings, and if I do not preserve the latter, I do not preserve myself." Maybe my grandmother was right: maybe cleanliness is next to godliness.

December 3: Life is the exercise in perpetual becoming. There is always someplace new to go, something new to learn, something new to appreciate.

December 4: Never doubt that all of life reflects the nature of God. Where else do we see the power of God more clearly than in the waves of the sea? Where else can we contemplate the beauty of God more specifically if not in a rose? Where else can we see the compassion of God if not in the eyes of the other?

December 5: "To live," Oscar Wilde wrote, "is the rarest thing in the world. Most people exist, that is all." It's a sad thought but perhaps a true one. In a culture dedicated to work, to money, and to things, we are often too busy to enjoy the world in which we exist. What a waste of creation.

December 6: Maybe Christmas is really about learning to appreciate the basics of life for what they are: the arenas in which we learn to distinguish early what is really important in life from what are merely its frills.

December 7: What we do not care for in creation we lose. We are losing at a great rate birds and fish and trees and also species of insects necessary to the survival of our crops. Real awareness of life, of incarnation, of the meaning of Christmas would change our commitment to consumption to a commitment to enoughness.

December 8: Gil Stern made the comment once that humans are very complex beings who "make deserts bloom and lakes die." The comment is a chilling one, not because it is true but because we seem to be able to do the one without even adverting to the effects of the other.

December 9: It's so easy to live cement and plastic lives in a world in which we spend our days rushing from the house to the car to the office. When was the last time you spent an hour outside in fresh air? If you're really looking for the presence of God, you might want to go where God is in forms of life other than our own.

December 10: "The ability of all creatures to share in the process of ongoing creation makes all things sacred," Paula Allen wrote. As long as we see life of any kind, we see God.

December 11: The arrogance of the human being is without bounds. Despite the fact that everything else in creation can survive without us, we fail to realize as we rape the earth to satisfy our runaway thirst for goods that we are totally dependent on the rest of nature. So when it runs out, what happens to us?

December 12: To go through life without ever being alive enough to sing the angels' song of awareness and crazy glee just at the thought of Life alive is not to have lived at all.

December 13: "There is a very fine line," Maya Angelou wrote, "between loving life and being greedy for it." Greed is the enemy of the Christmas spirit. A sense of enoughness is a gift to be cultivated all year round.

December 14: It is of the essence of human nature to want to live. Why do you suppose then that this desire does not seem to be the ultimate arbitrator of the choices we make, the way we live, the things we do, the resources we use? Maybe it's because being alive and learning to live are two different things.

December 15: We're born wailing while other people smile. But if we live life well, we die smiling while other people wail.

December 16: When we make the area in which we live clean, ordered, beautiful, simple, and steeped in nature we glorify the God of life who, in creation, did the same for us.

December 17: What is an inadequate life? It is any life lived out of touch with nature, with the rhythm of the day, with the seasons of the year, with the softness of water, the energy of fire, the clarity of air, the moisture of good earth. Anything else is not life. It is, at best, humanity prefabricated.

December 18: It is not possible to be fully human without coming to know, to respect, to learn from, the rest of life. We were not put on this earth alone. We were put here to grow in concert with everything else.

December 19: "Life," Samuel Butler said, "is like playing a violin solo in public and learning the instrument as one goes on." When you look at our high-rise cities, you know how much we have yet to learn.

December 20: To be a spectator at the game of life, to live only vicariously — through televisions and computers and self-contained neighborhoods and apartment buildings constructed to protect us from the world at large — is to forget that we were born to help complete the rest of creation.

December 21: When we manage to create for ourselves the perfect living space, uninterrupted and uninterruptable, we can be sure that we are no longer living life. "The eternal mistake of [hu]mankind,"

Aleister Crowley wrote, "is to set up an attainable ideal."

December 22: To make ourselves a world unto ourselves, without the solace of nature, is to be perpetually confronted with the spiritual impoverishment of the self alone.

December 23: To go through life with eyes half shut is to miss stars and angels everywhere. Within the stable of every experience God awaits us with new revelations about life.

December 24: To find ourselves alone in life, stripped of life's trappings and with nothing but the self, can be one of life's most gifting moments. Then we come to see the glories of God hidden in the secret places of time. Then we come to realize how graced we are just to have been born.

December 25: Christmas, the celebration of the birth of a child, is about the fact that God's presence is everywhere. In the smallest things. In the weakest things. In the beginning of things. And we are responsible for nurturing it.

December 26: When we use the globe as if it were a private preserve, we lose our right to a place in the universe. We were not put here to dominate. We were put here to be.

December 27: Any progress made without the defense of nature in mind is not progress at all.

December 28: Nature in all its fury, all its wildness, teaches us our limits. Human pride gives way to humility in the face of a single flower, a roaring wind, an erupting volcano. Nature saves us from the boundaries of the self.

December 29: Walt Whitman wrote: "After you have exhausted what there is in business, politics, conviviality, and so on — have found that none of these finally satisfy, or permanently wear — what remains? Nature remains." We are not "above" nature; we are part of nature. In that understanding may well lie the sanctity of the human race.

December 30: If you really want to give a gift worthy of Christmas, give respect for nature. It has so much to give us, so much to teach us. Or as the story goes:

Adam said, "God, I am very lonely now that you are not walking with me like you once did in the Garden."

And God said, "No problem. I'll make a new animal to walk with you to remind you of my love for you no matter what you do or how you act." And it was a good animal. And God was pleased and called it "dog" because it was a reflection of God's own love for Adam.

And Dog lived with Adam and loved him. And Adam was comforted. And God was pleased. And Dog was content and wagged its tail.

Then Adam's guardian angel came to God and said, "Adam is now filled with pride. Dog has indeed taught him that he is loved, but perhaps too well. He thinks he's worthy of adoration."

And God said, "No problem. I'll create for him a companion who will see him as he is. This new animal will remind him of his limitations." And so God created "cat."

And when Adam gazed into Cat's eyes, he was reminded that he was not the supreme being. And Adam learned humility.

And God was pleased. And Adam was greatly improved. And Dog was happy. And Cat didn't give a hoot one way or the other.

December 31: The year is over. We stand at a new moment in time. We can choose to go on as before, raping the globe, threatening the planet, making specimens of people, or we can melt into the grace of the universe and become what we were created to be, a family in harmony with itself.

Welcome to...

The Monastic Way

by Joan D. Chittister, O.S.B.

If you are a seeker of the sacred...
If spirituality is an important part of your life...
If you would like a daily companion along the way...

Subscribe to...

The Monastic Way

This monthly, single-page publication with daily reflections by one of today's most inspiring religious writers and speakers is ideal for:

- Personal daily reflection
- Homily starters
- Opening prayers for classes, meetings, group gatherings
- Faith sharing

$15 per year includes postage; add $3 for overseas mailing.

Send to *Benetvision,* 355 E. Ninth St., Erie, PA 16503-1107 or call (814) 459-5994. Fax: (814) 459-8066

Quantity discounts available upon request.

ORDER FORM for The Monastic Way
Use this order form for your personal subscription or gift subscriptions.

Name of recipient _____

Address _____

City _____ State _____ ZIP_____

Phone (_____)_____

If gift, name of sender _____

❒ $15 is enclosed for each subscription ($12 subscription + $3 postage).
(Please add an extra $3.00 for overseas mailing.)

❒ Quantity discounts are available upon request.

Mail to: *Benetvision,* 355 East Ninth St., Erie, PA 16503-1107
Phone (814) 459-5994   Fax (814) 459-8066